AUSTRALIA
dreaming

THE QUILTERS' GUILD *gratefully acknowledges the following: J.B. Fairfax Press Pty Limited, for their support for this project; Noel Frankham, for his foreword; the Lord Mayor of Sydney, Alderman Frank Sartor; the Lord Mayor of Nagoya, Takeyoshi Nishio; Carolyn Sullivan, for her introduction; Karen Fail, editor of the artists' statements; Meredith Hinchliffe, Helen Slocombe and Karen Fail, the selectors of the collection; and the members of the organising committee — Margaret Wright (chairman), Trudy Brodie, Lois Cook, Larraine Scouler, Choy-Lin Williams.*

EDITORIAL
Managing Editor: Judy Poulos
Editorial Assistant: Ella Martin
Editorial Coordinator: Margaret Kelly
Photography: Andrew Payne

DESIGN AND PRODUCTION
Manager: Anna Maguire
Layout: Lulu Dougherty
Picture Editor: Kirsten Holmes
Trainee Production Editor: Danielle Thiris

Published by J.B. Fairfax Press Pty Limited
80-82 McLachlan Ave
Rushcutters Bay, NSW 2011, Australia
A.C.N. 003 738 430

Printed by Toppan Printing Co, Singapore

JBFP 417

AUSTRALIA DREAMING
Quilts to Nagoya
ISBN 1 86343 247 7

AUSTRALIA
Quilts to Nagoya
dreaming

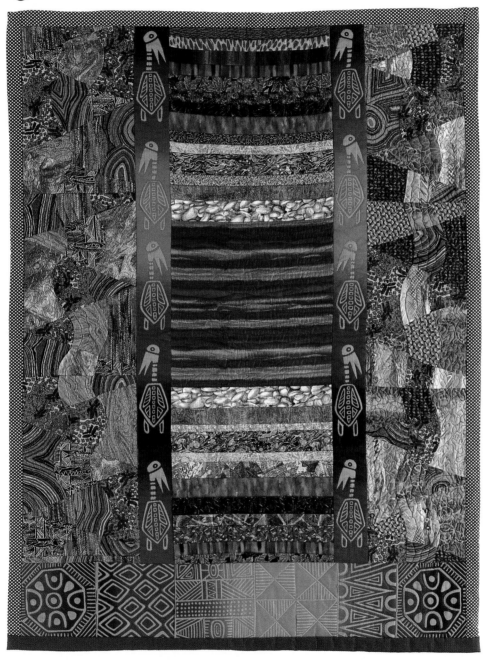

The Quilters' Guild Inc.

A J.B. Fairfax Press Publication

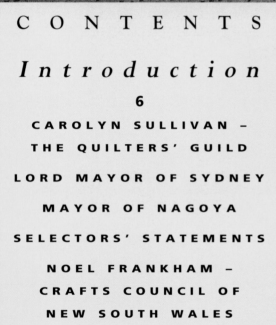

CONTENTS

Introduction

The invitation from Sydney City Council to The Quilters' Guild to participate in the Sydney Fair in Nagoya in October 1995 came as a result of the Colours of Australia quilts exhibition held at the Sydney Opera House in 1994. The request for the Sydney Fair was for a new collection of quilts which the Guild titles Australia Dreaming. Again, quiltmakers were challenged to create a new art quilt, reflecting images of Australia. This time, the quilts were destined for exhibition and sale in an international setting.

The opportunity to exhibit is very important to these quiltmakers. Seen in a prestigious arena, the work, which would generally be regarded as a domestic craft, is often judged to be more valuable and provides public recognition of the efforts of the quiltmaker. One indicator of how important such collections are to quiltmakers is shown by the huge response. Not only the professional quiltmakers, but also those who look on quiltmaking as a hobby or pastime, have been very quick to submit their quilt for inclusion in the collection.

Quiltmakers make quilts because they provide an artistic outlet using a medium that is soft, decorative and functional. Only a few quiltmakers consider themselves artistic, yet all produce beautiful art works which they use to decorate their homes, share with family and friends and, on occasion, exhibit. The selection of colour, design, texture and fabrics are all artistic decisions. While not everyone has their quilt selected for a juried collection such as this, it is the decision-making, effort and love which makes every quilt special.

The discipline required to make a quilt to a theme and to a particular size enables the quiltmakers to define their thoughts, refine their skills and to challenge themselves in a unique way. Many of the quiltmakers participating in Australia Dreaming willingly share their emotions about Australia through their quilts. Concern for the environment, despair over the drought, patriotism, as well as a quiet reflection on the beauty of our country, provide some of the themes.

A body of art quilts such as these has importance because it is so distinctively Australian. Such work is not to be seen elsewhere. However, The Quilters' Guild has a history of such collections, beginning with the highly successful Quilt Australia '88, then Quilts Covering Australia, a small exhibition that toured Australia and, most recently, the Colours of Australia exhibition that began its five-year tour of Australia in March 1995. Having the new collection, Australia Dreaming, seen in Nagoya is particularly exciting. The extent of Japanese tourism to Australia shows how much the Japanese people are interested in Australia and things Australian. They are particularly attracted by our wide open spaces. Australia is the same size as the United States, yet has a population the same as Greater Tokyo. The colour and light of Australia are also very distinctive. The quilts continually reinforce the very features that attract Japanese tourists to Australia.

In addition, Australians have always welcomed Japanese manufactured goods, and these have become such an integral part of our lives that we often do not recognise their country of origin. These trading relationships do not necessarily translate into an understanding of the values of individuals. It is hoped that Australian quilt-makers can further foster this understanding, through the artistic and emotional thoughts expressed in these quilts .

Australia Dreaming is a personal view of where we have come from, where we are going, what is and what could be. The quilt-makers have expressed these ideas by exploring new directions in quilt-making. Such success ensures that The Quilters' Guild has truly fulfilled its goals — to promote the art and craft of quiltmaking.

Carolyn Sullivan
President 1995
The Quilters' Guild

THE LORD MAYOR OF SYDNEY
COUNCILLOR FRANK SARTOR

TELEPHONE: (02) 265 9229
FAX: (02) 265 9328

THE TOWN HALL
SYDNEY 2000
AUSTRALIA

MESSAGE FROM THE LORD MAYOR

Sydney City Council is delighted that the Quilters' Guild will be participating in the Sydney Fair in Nagoya in October 1995.

The Sydney Fair is the most ambitious project to be undertaken by one of Sydney's Sister City Committees and will promote both the city's business activities as well as cultural projects. The Fair marks the 15th Anniversary of the Sydney-Nagoya Sister City relationship.

The Quilters' Guild project, *Australia Dreaming*, exhibits the high level of creativity, skill and sophistication that is found in the craft work now produced in this country. The quilts themselves represent the Australian development of a textile art form which has its roots in many different cultures.

I congratulate the Quilters' Guild for so successfully undertaking the *Australia Dreaming* project and for exhibiting it in the Sydney Fair in Nagoya.

City of Nagoya

CITY HALL

1-1, SANNOMARU 3-CHOME, NAKA-KU
NAGOYA 400-08, JAPAN

TAKEYOSHI NISHIO
MAYOR

On behalf of the City of Nagoya, it is my great pleasure to
welcome the participants of the Sydney Fair.

This fair is being held to mark the 15th anniversary of the
signing of the sister city partnership between the cities of
Sydney and Nagoya in 1980. Over the years great strides have
been made in the furthering of mutual understanding and
friendship through exchanges in fields as diverse as trade,
education and culture.

The City of Nagoya is delighted that the Quilters' Guild
exhibition of quilts, "Australia Dreaming", is to be part of
the Sydney Fair. The Japanese have a great appreciation for
textile arts and indeed Nagoya itself is home to the renowned
Arimatsu Shibori technique for tie-dying cloth. Also, while
nowadays the Nagoya economic region is famous for its
automobiles, it was actually the birthplace of the automatic
loom and a thriving centre of the textile industry. I feel
that this exhibition pinpoints an area of mutual interest and
therefore provides an ideal opportunity to strengthen our
sister city ties.

I would like to offer my sincerest thanks to the Quilters'
Guild for bringing this art form to Nagoya. I am sure that
the exhibits will prove a great source of interest for the
local people and heighten our awareness of the treasures of
Australia.

Takeyoshi Nishio
Mayor
City of Nagoya

Selectors' Statements

Although Australia has many cultures enriching its population, man is still swamped by the enormous isolation and the tyranny of distance of this timeless country. We are indeed fringe dwellers whether it be the fringe of the sea, the desert, or the rest of the world. Our lives are intensely influenced by the often violent extremes of seasons. There is desolation and there is abundance. Our attitudes are changing from the concept of conquering the land to the Aboriginal belief that we and nature are one with the land.

These quilts communicate this symbolism with clear expression, understanding and judgment of design and colour. The message and technique are the means to the end, which is to encourage the viewer to recognise that intangible Australian spirit.

In some quilts, the message is graphic and easily recognised, while in others the message is abstract, touching an inner response. The techniques involve printing, painting, dyeing and cyanotyping fabric, adding texture with fraying, layering, stitching and quilting. Where traditional piecing is used, an Australian emotion has been added by means of colour, vibrating and pulsing or quietly reflecting earth and rock tones. The fabrics show patterns from Europe, America, Asian batiks and Aboriginal and Islander prints, reflecting our multicultural base. There is confidence and there is a strong energy.

It seems significant that although the quilters have come from different social backgrounds, this is not accented. The land has drawn us in. We are reaching back with the help of Aboriginal art and legends to the bones and soul of our country — the Spirit of the Dreaming.

Helen Slocombe

It is always an honour to be included among the selectors of an exhibition, especially one which is destined to have international exposure. Australia Dreaming promised to be an exciting collection of small quilts and I had expectations of seeing many images with a distinctly Australian theme. I was not disappointed. All the quilts submitted for selection were viewed as an entire collection and gave us an opportunity to appreciate the diversity of themes and the variety of techniques used to interpret these themes. The most common theme chosen by the quilt artists was the land and our connection to it. Whether using traditional piecing as a background to very Australian images, as in Julie Woods' 'Outback Splendour', or the simple landscape of Choy-Lin Williams's 'Outback Traffic Jam', each quiltmaker sought to convey reactions to and thoughts about this land, Australia. When selecting the final forty-five quilts, we looked for excellence in technique, well-balanced design, successful colour combinations, and quilts that truly reflected the title of the exhibition — Australia Dreaming. The collection also needed to be balanced, providing the viewer with an insight into quiltmaking in Australia in all its facets. New techniques, such as wool yarn couching in Judy Turner's 'Desert Sky' and the use of felted 'rag' in Glenys Mann's 'Postcard — Wish You Were Here', provide a creative juxtaposition for quilts with a more traditional starting point, such as Kerry Gadd's 'Heat Wave' and Betty O'Brien's 'Land of Many Splendours'.

It was obvious that many quiltmakers had used this exhibition as an opportunity to expand and experiment with their quiltmaking, providing us all with an exciting collection of quilts. Congratulations to all and to The Quilters' Guild for continuing to provide such opportunities to Australian quiltmakers.

Karen Fail

I was delighted to be invited to be a participant in the selection of a body of quilts to go to Japan. What impacted most on me was the strong use of colour representing the Australian environment. The heat and rich red shimmer of northern Australia, the dusty brown and grey of the dry, the delicate colours of the sky and earth when the wet comes, and the bright colours of the coastline are all shown in the quilts in this exhibition. The quilts demonstrate a masterful use and understanding of colour.

The other important thing for me was the adaptation of traditional patchwork patterns. Australian quilters use these patterns as a starting point, a means to an end. Many explore the qualities of fabric and combine these with colour and design to express their feelings about the country in which we live. There is a huge diversity in the techniques used by the quiltmakers on show.

These quilts are uniquely Australian. The colours, the fabrics and the patterns combine to give them life and vitality. I believe they convey the 'essence' of Australia.

The quilts show a maturity and originality in design which is very exciting.

Meredith Hinchliffe

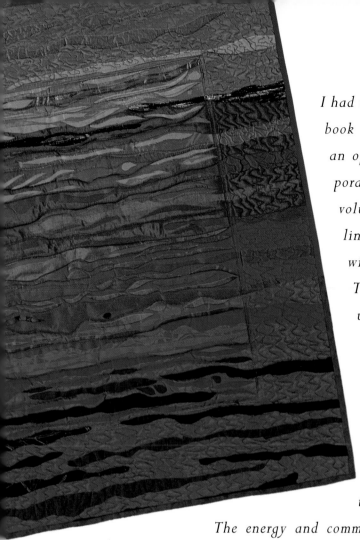

I had the great pleasure of launching The Quilters' Guild book Colours of Australia *in March 1995. It gave me an opportunity to acknowledge the strength of contemporary Australian quilting, and to praise the effort of a volunteer organisation in making the book and travelling exhibition happen. That exhibition of forty works will tour regional Australia for the next five years.*

The deeply personal nature of quilts is crucial to understanding their value. They have a cultural significance that allows them a very special and often critical role. Not unlike photographs, with which we all feel familiar, quilts have a capacity to touch the heart. We feel comfortable looking at them and we are then often surprised to discover that they deal with personal or socially provocative information.

The energy and commitment that resulted in Colours of Australia *is again being applied by The Quilters' Guild to an imaginative and exciting project.* Australia Dreaming *is a timely introduction to issues of the Australian psyche and environment.*

Most Australians claim a special relationship with place, whether it be rural, outback, urban or coastal. The works in the Australia Dreaming *collection present potent perspectives on many of the elements and issues facing Australians.*

NOEL FRANKHAM – CRAFTS COUNCIL OF NEW SOUTH WALES

Issues such as drought and the harsh environment for many inland dwellers are discussed in works such as Joan Apel's 'Australia All Over' and Judy Hooworth's 'Waiting for the Rains'. As Hooworth says: 'Its (the land's) raw beauty is deeply embedded in the hearts and souls of Australians'. The stresses imposed by a harsh land encourage an empathy that is a genuine and deeply felt emotion shared by new as well as the first (indigenous) Australians.

Heather Rose, with her quilt, 'Australian nexus – Dreamtime, Direction, Destiny', worries that urban Australians do not strive hard enough for harmony between cities and nature.

Carolyn Swart's 'Together – Let us Keep it Together' reminds us of the effort we owe the land if it

is to survive our intervention.
While the spirituality of Jan Irvine's
'Out of Gondwana' ponders the
'unfathomable depth of time', it
succinctly encapsulates the quality
and the ideas of all the quilts
included in the project.
For the second time this year
The Quilters' Guild has provided a vital and vigorous
account of Australian quilters. 'Australia Dreaming
– Quilts to Nagoya' is
a testament to the skill
and talent of the
quiltmakers and the
dedication of the
organisers.
All the quilts in
Australia Dreaming consider in a
very serious way some of the key issues
challenging Australians and all
peoples of the earth. While there is a
specificity to Australia within the
quilts illustrated in this fine book,
there is a universality that will ensure
that they are meaningful to a very
wide audience.

Noel Frankham
General Manager
Crafts Council of New South Wales

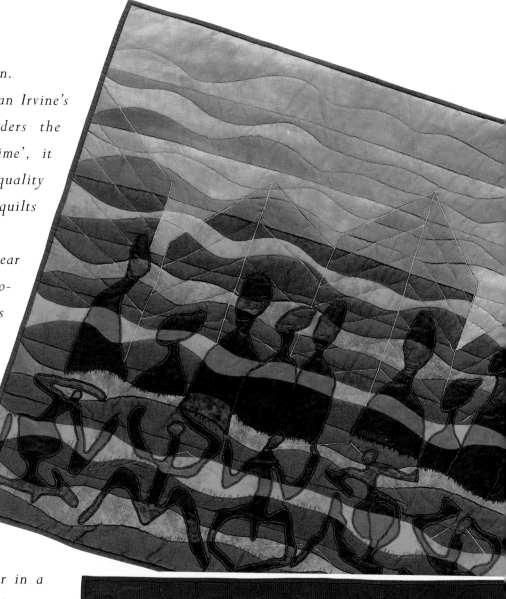

The strong vibrant colours of the Australian outback reflect the strong characters of the people on the land, who are all still pioneers at heart.

JOAN APEL

Port Hedland, Western Australia

AUSTRALIA ALL OVER
SIZE: 90 CM X 125 CM
MATERIALS: COTTON, ORGANZA, VELVET
TECHNIQUES: MACHINE-PIECING, MACHINE-
QUILTING, EMBELLISHED TEXTURED SURFACE

Over the years, many people have come to Australia because they were following a dream for a better place, a free place, a different place, an opportunity for a fresh start. Can we, like the resilient dragonfly, hold onto our dream and adapt to the changes facing us with the disappearing natural environment and growing cultural diversity?

DEBORAH BREARLEY

Queenscliff, Victoria

HOLDING ON
SIZE: 99 CM X 105 CM
MATERIALS: HAND-DYED, HAND-PRINTED AND
CYANOTYPE COTTON FABRICS
TECHNIQUES: MACHINE-PIECING, MACHINE-
QUILTING, PAINTING AND EMBELLISHING

I made this quilt while on board our yacht anchored in Gove harbour in the Northern Territory, capturing Mother Nature's display in the sky during the wet season.

CATHERINE BROWN
Malaysia/Glen Iris, Victoria

THE WET – NORTH-EAST ARNHEMLAND
SIZE: 91 CM X 125 CM
MATERIALS: CALICO, COTTON, SILK, MOHAIR,
SILK ORGANZA
TECHNIQUES: HAND-PAINTING, HAND-
QUILTING, MACHINE-PIECING

Australians dream of their sacred leisure time and enjoy sporting and cultural activities. Our glorious busy harbour, the ferries and Sunday yacht races blend with the Opera House 'sails' and epitomise this dream.

DALE BROWN

Nowra, New South Wales

SUNDAYS ON SYDNEY HARBOUR
SIZE: 91 CM X 98 CM
MATERIAL: COTTON
TECHNIQUES: HAND-PIECING, MACHINE-
PIECING, CRAZY QUILTING

Although I live in the south of the continent, the essence of Australia is more apparent in the centre and north. Ancient and very often inhospitable, these areas are part of our past, present and future, to be cherished for their landforms and wildlife.

EILEEN CAMPBELL

Kew, Victoria

DANCE OF THE BROLGAS
SIZE: 140 CM X 143 CM
MATERIALS: COTTON, BLENDS
TECHNIQUES: ALL MACHINE WORK

I want people to feel they are part of the landscape — to reach out and touch the beautiful colours of the sunset, to touch Mother Earth and to know we are responsible for her preservation.

ELAINE CAMPBELL

Arana Hills, Queensland

THE SPIRIT OF THE AUSTRALIAN OUTBACK
SIZE: 90 CM X 125 CM
MATERIALS: PAINTED, DYED AND
MANIPULATED FABRICS
TECHNIQUES: EMBROIDERY AND QUILTING

The windmill offers a clean alternative energy source and heralds our changing attitudes to our world. It highlights the need for us to be continually vigilant to protect our world.

DIJANNE CEVAAL

Fairfield, Victoria

WINDS OF CHANGE
SIZE: 116 CM X 134 CM
MATERIALS: HAND-DYED COTTONS, LINOCUT
PRINTED FABRIC
TECHNIQUES: MACHINE-PIECING, MACHINE-
QUILTING, APPLIQUE

The structure of the quilt is inspired by the Japanese Rising Sun; rivers flow towards a central billabong, and vibrant segments represent many cultures that make up the Australian identity.

DIANNE FINNEGAN

Lane Cove, New South Wales

JAMBOREE

SIZE: 125 CM X 140 CM

MATERIAL: COTTON

TECHNIQUES: MACHINE-PIECING,

MACHINE-QUILTING

My quilt pays homage to the lost art of making possum-skin cloaks and mats. The quilting pattern makes reference to the contours of the landscape, and the applied colour is reminiscent of the ochres used to colour the original possum-skin cloaks.

DIANNE FIRTH

Turner, Australian Capital Territory

POSSUM-SKIN DREAMING
SIZE: 90 CM X 119 CM
MATERIALS: POLYESTER/VISCOSE, COTTON
TECHNIQUES: MACHINE-PIECING,
MACHINE-QUILTING

After a fortnight of continuously high tem-
peratures, the heat appeared to shimmer like a
mirage. With Australia's diverse beauty, I am
never short of design inspirations.

KERRY GADD

Tintaldra, Victoria

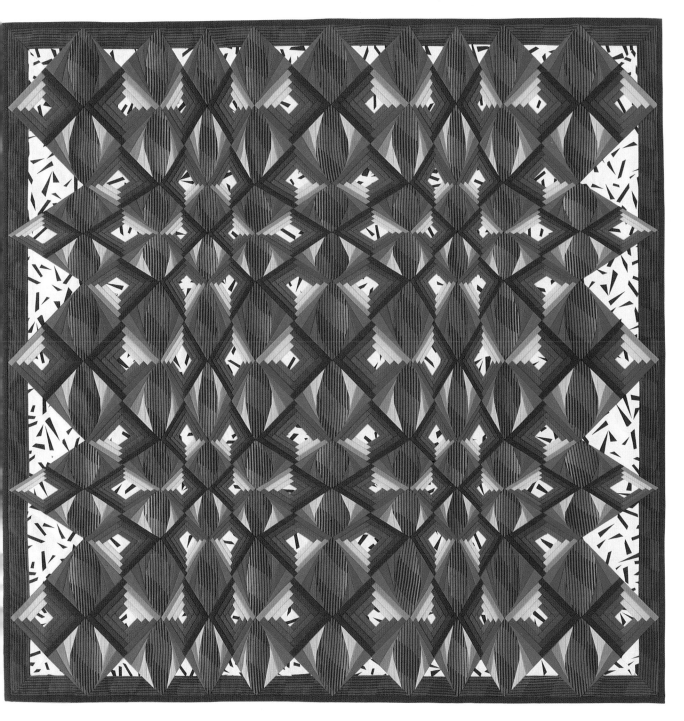

HEAT WAVE
SIZE: 109 CM X 109 CM
MATERIAL: COTTON
TECHNIQUE: MACHINE-PIECING ONTO A
PERMANENT FOUNDATION

Living on fifty acres in the bush, it is almost inevitable that I create landscape quilts. The piecing structure of this quilt refers to rock formations with the soft Australian colours adding a dreamlike quality.

FIONA GAVENS
Grafton, New South Wales

DREAMSCAPE
SIZE: 96 CM X 130 CM
MATERIALS: HAND-PAINTED SILK,
PRINTED FABRIC BY VIVIEN HALEY
TECHNIQUES: MACHINE-PIECING,
HAND-QUILTING

With Australian wildflowers as my source of inspiration, I have taken traditional quilting forms and interpreted them using modern techniques and Australian themes.

JANE GIBSON

Epping, New South Wales

WILDFLOWER REVERIE
SIZE: 110 CM X 110 CM
MATERIALS: SILK FABRIC, METALLIC THREAD
TECHNIQUES: MACHINE-PIECING,
MACHINE-QUILTING

The discovery of the wonderfully coloured desert pea conjured up visions of a desert centre, windblown dust and sand, stunted vegetation and then the revelation of these brilliant red, black-centred flowers.

EVELYN GRAY

North Rocks, New South Wales

STURT'S DESERT PEA

SIZE: 107 CM X 108 CM

MATERIALS: COTTON, EMBROIDERY
AND METALLIC THREADS

TECHNIQUES: MACHINE-PIECING,
MACHINE-QUILTING

I wanted to capture the spectacular colour of the sun setting in the Hamersley Range in Western Australia, using traditional quilting blocks and scrap fabrics rather than a pictorial image.

ANN HADDAD

Canberra, Australian Capital Territory

HAMERSLEY SUNSET
SIZE: 123 CM X 125 CM
MATERIAL: COTTON
TECHNIQUES: MACHINE-PIECING,
MACHINE-QUILTING

My quilt is inspired by images of the vast, dry areas of Australia — straight, red rutted roads, old mountain ranges, layered rock faces, monoliths and gorges, dead trees and the occasional line of greenery.

CAROL HEATH

Ballarat, Victoria

DRY LAND, MY LAND
SIZE: 90 CM X 123 CM
MATERIAL: COTTON
TECHNIQUES: PHOTO TRANSFER, MACHINE-
APPLIQUE, MACHINE-PIECING, HAND-
QUILTING, MACHINE-QUILTING

The huge sky, the sparseness of vegetation and the harsh contrasts of colour in this land, Australia, create a strange emotional pull to the outback — even for city dwellers. The hand-painted fabrics suggested drought to me and provided the inspiration for 'Waiting for the Rains'.

JUDY HOOWORTH
Terrey Hills, New South Wales

WAITING FOR THE RAINS
SIZE: 141 CM X 148 CM
MATERIALS: COTTONS AND BLENDS
(SOME HAND-DYED FABRICS BY GLENDA
MORGAN AND ALVENA HALL)
TECHNIQUES: MACHINE-PIECING,
HAND-QUILTING, MACHINE-QUILTING

The ancient land mass of Gondwana conjures up ideas of origin and unfathomable depth of time. The spiralling path, connecting earth and stars, provides an analogy for humanity and for man's spiritual relationship with the environment.

JAN IRVINE

Gulgong, New South Wales

OUT OF GONDWANA
SIZE: 90 CM X 147 CM
MATERIALS: SILK, WOOL FILLING
TECHNIQUES: AIRBRUSH DYEING,
HAND-QUILTING

Inspired by the sea viewed from my studio window, I wanted to capture this ever-changing environment, using colour to create illusionary effects.

PAM JONES

Wallaroo, South Australia

AUSTRALIAN NEXUS — DREAMTIME, DIRECTION, DESTINY
SIZE: 102 CM X 125 CM
MATERIAL: COTTON
TECHNIQUES: HAND-DYEING, CYANOTYPING, HAND-
PIECING, MACHINE-PIECING, APPLIQUE, MACHINE-
EMBROIDERY, MACHINE-QUILTING

Avoca was my brother-in-law's sheep station,
sold in 1994 because of the drought. The dry
baked earth killed everything around it, yet
maintained a cruel beauty not to be forgotten.

DEBORAH LOUIE
Jannali, New South Wales

REMEMBER AVOCA
SIZE: 98 CM X 127 CM
MATERIAL: COTTON
TECHNIQUES: HAND-DYEING, MACHINE-
PIECING, MACHINE-QUILTING

Unlike the original inhabitants, who lived in harmony with the harsh conditions of Australia's great red interior, most modern Australians crowd onto the coastline and look outwards to the sea — true fringe dwellers.

WENDY LUGG

Bullcreek, Western Australia

FRINGE DWELLERS
SIZE: 106 CM X 118 CM
MATERIALS: SILK, COTTON,
FABRIC-PRINTING INK
TECHNIQUES: MACHINE-PIECING,
MACHINE-EMBROIDERY, MACHINE-QUILTING

Many of my quilts are inspired by the Australian landscape. This one is in the colours of our wild flowers, some subtle some quite garish, all under a blue sky.

BARBARA MACEY

Mount Waverley, Victoria

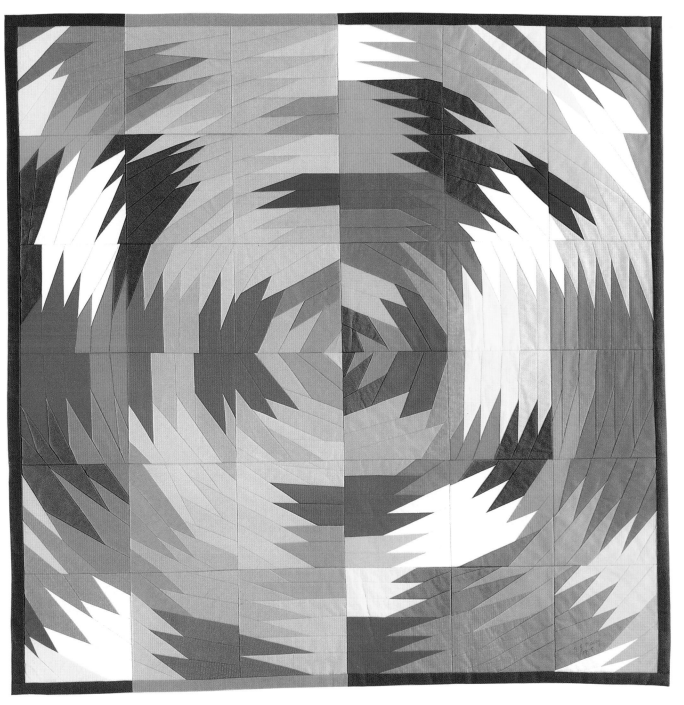

WILD FLOWERS AND BLUE SKY
SIZE: 111 CM X 112 CM
MATERIALS: COTTON, COTTON BLENDS,
PELLON BATTING
TECHNIQUES: FOUNDATION-PIECING, TYING

My camera is my best friend when I travel. With it I can take back with me all the hues and feelings — not only of the country but of the people as well. Just like on a postcard, there is never enough room to encourage every-one to fulfil their dreams.

GLENYS MANN

Tamworth, New South Wales

POSTCARD — WISH YOU WERE HERE
SIZE: 90 CM X 147 CM
MATERIALS: COTTON, COTTON AND
SILK THREADS
TECHNIQUES: FELTED 'RAG' EMBELLISHMENT,
MACHINE-QUILTING

This quilt is inspired by the Tiwi women of Bathurst and Melville islands who printed the fabrics. The designs represent aspects of Tiwi life — the environment, ceremonies and daily events.

JUDY McDERMOTT

Thornleigh, New South Wales

PINK IS FOR GIRLS
SIZE: 111 CM X 143 CM
MATERIALS: COTTON, SILK, RAYON,
VARIOUS THREADS
TECHNIQUES: HAND-STITCHING,
MACHINE-STITCHING

On a trip to the Kimberley region of Western Australia, I was greeted by this view of the Chamberlain River, alive with rainbow bee-eaters flying in profusion to greet me as I woke each day.

CYNTHIA MORGAN
Caloundra, Queensland

KIMBERLEY DREAMING
SIZE: 98 CM X 118 CM
MATERIALS: COTTON, SILK, ORGANZA, LINEN
TECHNIQUES: HAND-DYEING,
PAINTING, EMBROIDERY

The images and uninhibited movement of the
Aboriginal figures are set against a backdrop
of rock caverns and ever-changing shadows.

ROSLYN MOULES
Bonnet Bay, New South Wales

INNER SENSATIONS OF SPIRIT BEINGS
SIZE: 94 CM X 148 CM
MATERIALS: COTTON, ORGANZA
TECHNIQUES: MACHINE-PIECING,
MACHINE-QUILTING

My inspiration is the marine environment around Australia, an island where most people live on the coast. I find the water very calming and refreshing.

ALISON MUIR

Neutral Bay, New South Wales

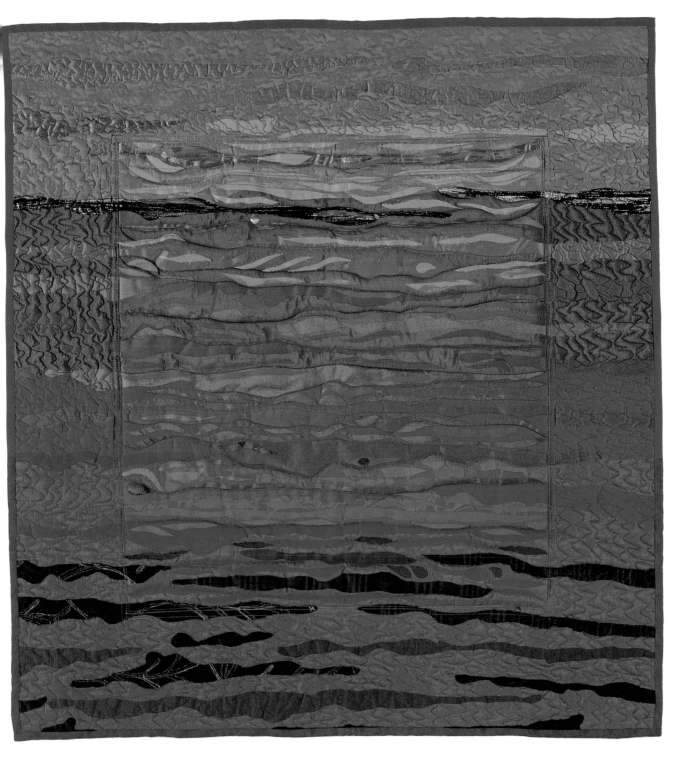

REFLECTIONS OF A COASTAL DWELLER
SIZE: 90 CM X 96 CM
MATERIALS: SILK, POLYESTER
TECHNIQUES: APPLIQUE, MACHINE-QUILTING

The quilt is a tribute to the courage and resilience of country people during drought. The green border signifies the ever-present hope of life-giving rains.

VAL NADIN

Pennant Hills, New South Wales

THE BIG DRY
SIZE: 124 CM X 136 CM
MATERIAL: COTTON (COMMERCIAL AND
HAND-DYED)
TECHNIQUES: HAND-DYEING, MACHINE-
PIECING, MACHINE-QUILTING

When I swam for the first time in the warm sunny waters of the Great Barrier Reef, it was all I had hoped for — full of spectacular fish and sea life. My visit inspired me to use the watery pattern of Snail Trail to reflect the rhythm of the sea and to suggest the warmth and excitement of the Reef, from its shadowy depths to the sunlit surface.

FELICITY NAESS

Wentworth Falls, New South Wales

CORAL REEF
SIZE: 102 CM X 144 CM
MATERIAL: COTTON
TECHNIQUES: MACHINE-PIECING, HAND-QUILTING

My favourite poem, My Country, by Dorothea Mackellar, had to be included in this quilt. It is enhanced by the tranquil scene from a watercolour painted by my father-in-law in 1924.

Permission for the use of My Country granted by the copyright holders, care of Curtis Brown (Australia) Pty Limited Sydney.

BETTY O'BRIEN

Mount Gambier, South Australia

LAND OF MANY SPLENDOURS
SIZE: 92 CM X 103 CM
MATERIALS: COTTON, POLYESTER
TECHNIQUES: HAND-PIECING, MACHINE-PIECING,
HAND-EMBROIDERY, MACHINE-APPLIQUE

On entering Kata Tjuta, I felt I was visiting a special place. A type of shyness came over me and I felt a presence there of something not quite tangible.

ROSEMARY PENFOLD

Brisbane, Queensland

SETTING SHADOWS: ULURU AND KATA TJUTA
SIZE: 110 CM X 128 CM
MATERIALS: COTTON, LAME
TECHNIQUES: MACHINE-PIECING,
MACHINE-QUILTING

The wind whips up the oceans along the south-eastern seaboard, heading for the 'red centre'. My quilt depicts this image, with details embroidered on the surface to complete the story.

JO PETHERBRIDGE
Asquith, New South Wales

FROM THE SEA TO THE CENTRE
SIZE: 116 CM X 124 CM
MATERIAL: COTTON BLEND
TECHNIQUES: MACHINE-EMBROIDERY,
APPLIQUE, MACHINE-QUILTING

Living in south-east Queensland and witnessing the urban encroachment on the vegetation due to progress, inspired me to interpret the loss of our ancestor's dream, from the Aboriginal dreamtime to the settler's dream of a new country, to urbanisation.

The quotation on the quilt is from the *200 Years Series*, published by Bay Books, courtesy Harper Collins Publishers.

LARAINE PICKETT

Carrara, Queensland

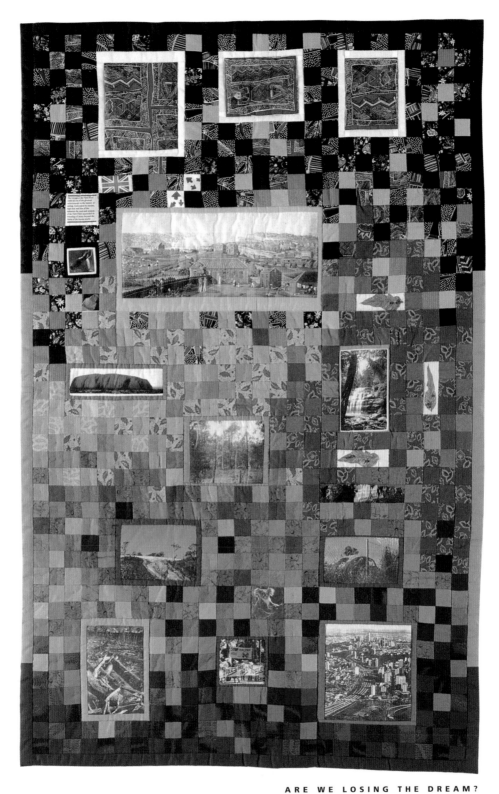

ARE WE LOSING THE DREAM?
SIZE: 93 CM X 143 CM
MATERIAL: COTTON
TECHNIQUES: PHOTO-IMAGING ONTO MATERIAL,
MACHINE-PIECING, HAND-QUILTING, PAINT
AND BEAD EMBELLISHMENT

The majority of Australians live by the sea so we must continually strive for harmony between our cities and nature. My quilt shows our architecture during lean and prosperous times, and the translucent water, clean and pollution-free.

HEATHER ROSE

Flagstaff Hill, South Australia

STATE OF TRANSITION
SIZE: 90 CM X 105 CM
MATERIALS: HAND-DYED AND COMMERCIAL
COTTONS
TECHNIQUES: HAND-APPLIQUÉ, MACHINE-
PIECING, MACHINE-QUILTING

Reflecting on a holiday at Birthday Station,
an old sheep station in South Australia, I
observed the remnants of human habitation
and the return of the native vegetation,
bringing back the birds, lizards and kan-
garoos to their natural habitat.

QUENBY SINCLAIR

McLaren Vale, South Australia

BIRTHDAY SHEEP STATION — RETURNING TO THE BUSH
SIZE: 114 CM X 122 CM
MATERIAL: COTTON
TECHNIQUES: PHOTO-TRANSFER, MACHINE-APPLIQUE,
MACHINE-PIECING, MACHINE-QUILTING

This quilt is inspired by the colours and shapes of the Kimberley landscape in remote north-west Australia. The area is a wilderness of diverse natural beauty with ancient rock formations, remarkable Aboriginal art and unique wildlife.

PAMELA SLATER

Mosman, New South Wales

KIMBERLEY PALETTE
SIZE: 106 CM X 140 CM
MATERIALS: COTTON, INCLUDING TIWI FABRICS
FROM MELVILLE ISLAND
TECHNIQUES: MACHINE-PIECING, HAND-QUILTING,
MACHINE-QUILTING

While our society is in a state of continual change, the land remains constant. I was inspired to make this quilt after seeing a photograph of New England National Park taken from Point Lookout. This view has been there for thousands of years and will be there for thousands more.

ADINA SULLIVAN
South Grafton, New South Wales

HORIZON
SIZE: 93 CM X 98 CM
MATERIALS: COTTONS (SOME HAND-DYED BY
HELEN BROOK), GOLD LAME
TECHNIQUES: MACHINE-PIECING,
MACHINE-QUILTING

With the abundance of wealth in this land, I tried to depict the vast fortune we have exploding from the earth, with our people all joined in harmony, sharing the bounty of this wonderful country.

CAROLYN SWART

Turramurra, New South Wales

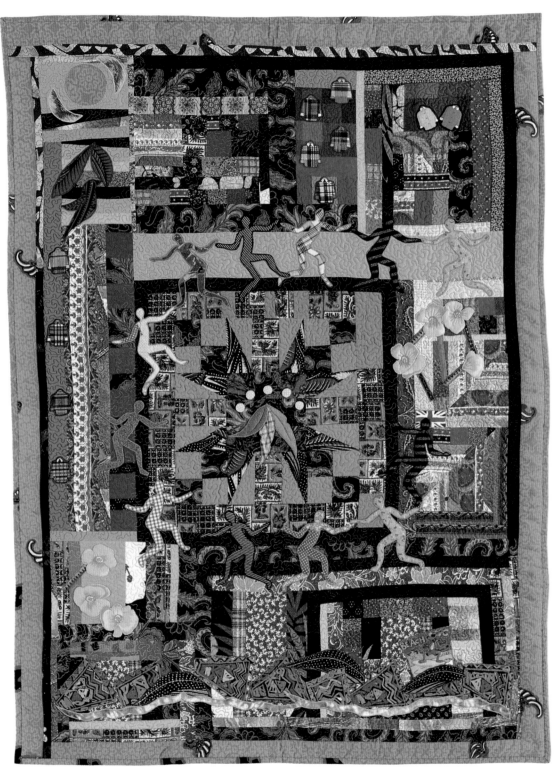

TOGETHER – LET US KEEP IT TOGETHER
SIZE: 100 CM X 135 CM
MATERIALS: COMMERCIAL AND HAND-DYED
COTTON AND BLEND FABRICS
TECHNIQUES: MACHINE-PIECING,
MACHINE-QUILTING

The vibrant colours of my quilt represent the centre of Australia, vast and mysterious yet full of excitement to be experienced by those who visit this area.

JAN TREGOWETH

Mount Gambier, South Australia

SUNBURNT COUNTRY
SIZE: 102 CM X 141 CM
MATERIAL: COTTON
TECHNIQUES: EMBROIDERY, SPRAY PAINT,
MACHINE-QUILTING, BURNT EDGES

The inspiration for 'Desert Sky' came from my memory of the colours of inland Australia. Although the land is vast and rich in colour, it is still overwhelmed by the clear blue sky.

JUDY TURNER

Chapman, Australian Capital Territory

DESERT SKY
SIZE: 90 CM X 106 CM
MATERIALS: WOOL FABRIC AND YARN
TECHNIQUES: MACHINE-PIECING,
MACHINE-QUILTING

This quilt was inspired by the dreamtime ancestral figures. According to the Koori, the Wandjina come out of the sky. They bring with them the rains, control the elements and maintain the fertility of the land.

SUE WADEMAN
Springwood, New South Wales

DESERT DREAMS — WANDJINA
SIZE: 90 CM X 112 CM
MATERIALS: SILK CHIFFON, SILK ORGANZA
TECHNIQUES: SILK-SCREEN PRINTING,
'PAINTING WITH THREADS',
FABRIC MANIPULATION

Australia Dreaming leaves a quiet yet power-ful imprint with the phases of the dreaming depicted in colour: ochre, reflecting our ancient history; gold, the era of wealth; and touches of blue which remind us of the need for clear blue skies.

CAROL WILKES
Winmalee, New South Wales

OH SO BOLD WE DREAM OF GOLD
SIZE: 116 CM X 145 CM
MATERIALS: COTTON, SILK ORGANZA, DYED SHIBORI
TECHNIQUE: FREE MACHINE-QUILTING

Outback Australia is my favourite holiday destination. In my quilt, I try to convey the feeling of space, solitude and timelessness.

CHOY-LIN WILLIAMS

Kurrajong Heights, New South Wales

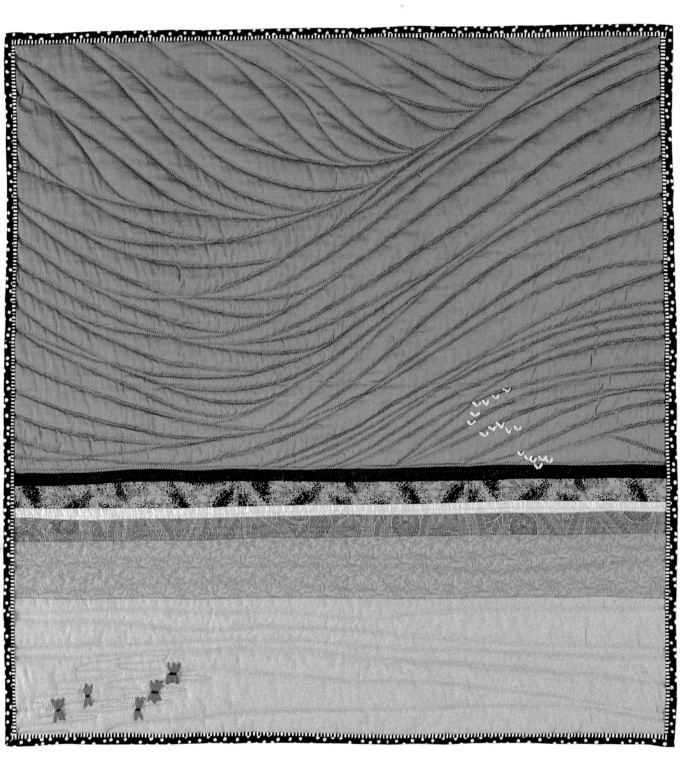

OUTBACK TRAFFIC JAM
SIZE: 92 CM X 96 CM
MATERIALS: COTTON, SILK FABRIC, SILK RIBBON
TECHNIQUES: HAND-APPLIQUE, HAND-QUILTING

To me, living in Australia means living in a diverse and exciting country. I have tried to create a feeling of the excitement of Australia, with colours permeating through each other, and a sense of dreaming by using a spiralling shifting design.

ELISABETH WILSON

Toowoomba, Queensland

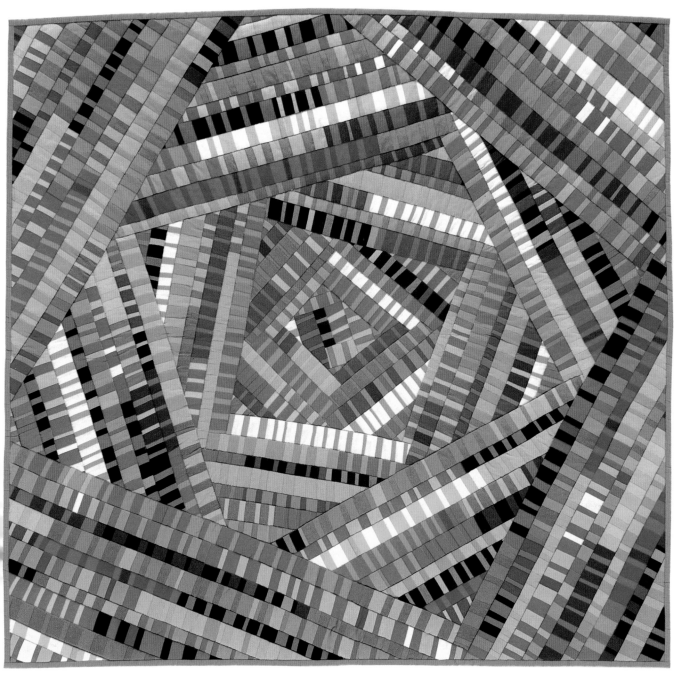

OZ-MOSIS
SIZE: 103 CM X 107 CM
MATERIALS: COTTON, COTTON BLENDS
TECHNIQUES: MACHINE-PIECING,
MACHINE-QUILTING

Man must live as one with the land. Finding a balance between progress and integration with the environment is an ongoing concern.

PAM WINSEN
Yeronga, Queensland

EPOCHS
SIZE: 99 CM X 121 CM
MATERIALS: HAND-DYED COTTON, ORGANZA, NET
TECHNIQUES: MACHINE-PIECING, APPLIQUE WITH
HANDMADE BRAID EDGE, MACHINE-EMBROIDERY,
MACHINE-QUILTING

On a windless day the depth of silence in the Australian outback is very soothing, providing a space in which the mind can expand and thoughts become attuned to the vast spaces of the land.

JULIE WOODS
Epping, New South Wales

OUTBACK SPLENDOUR
SIZE: 131 CM X 149 CM
MATERIAL: COTTON
TECHNIQUE: FOUNDATION-PIECING

Quiltmakers